Jewish
Festival Tales

written by

illustrated by

Saviour Pirotta

Anne Marie Kelly

RAINTREE
STECK-VAUGHN
RSVP PUBLISHERS

A Harcourt Company

Austin   New York
www.steck-vaughn.com

Festival Tales

Christian Festival Tales • Hindu Festival Tales
Jewish Festival Tales • Muslim Festival Tales

Published by Raintree Steck-Vaughn Publishers,
an imprint of Steck-Vaughn Company

Library of Congress Cataloging-in-Publication Data
Pirotta, Saviour.
Jewish festival tales / Saviour Pirotta; illustrated by Anne Marie Kelly.
p.   cm.—(Festival tales)
Includes bibliographical references and index.
ISBN 0-7398-2733-2
1. Fasts and feasts—Judaism—Juvenile literature.
2. Legends, Jewish.
3. Jews—Folklore.
[1. Fasts and feasts—Judaism. 2. Jews—Folklore. 3. Folklore.]
I. Kelly, Anne Marie, ill. II. Title. III. Series.
BM690.P57 2000
296.4'3—dc21   00-036938

Printed in Italy. Bound in the United States.
1 2 3 4 5 6 7 8 9 0 05 04 03 02 01

Contents

Heavens Above!

*The Jewish New Year starts with a ten-day period called the
High Holy Days. The first two days see the celebration of
Rosh Hashanah while the tenth day is called Yom Kippur.
Here's a Rosh Hashanah and Yom Kippur story from Eastern Europe.*

It was the night of Yom Kippur and the people in the town of Nemirov were hurrying to the synagogue. But where was the Rabbi? And how could they start their prayers without him?

"Every year, at this hour, he seems to disappear into thin air," said an old lady.

"They say he goes to heaven," said her friend, "to thank God personally for a good Rosh Hashanah and to make sure we have a happy new year."

One of the local boys scoffed at the women's talk. How could someone go to heaven without dying? No, the rabbi was disappearing somewhere else. Perhaps he was going to sleep when he should be praying. The boy decided to find out.

He crept out of the synagogue and into the rabbi's house next door. The rabbi, who trusted everyone, never locked his door. The boy hid under the bed. Some time later the rabbi came in. He went straight to the closet and put on some well-worn clothes: a pair of patched trousers, a thick sweater full of holes, and woodcutters' boots. Then he took an ax from the kitchen and set out once again.

The boy followed him, keeping in the shadows so he wouldn't be seen. At last the rabbi reached the nearby woods. Huffing and grunting, he felled an old, dead tree and chopped it into firewood. The boy saw him tie up the wood into a bundle and hurry back with it to town.

The rabbi knocked on the window of an old hut.

"Who is it?" called a woman's voice from inside.

"It is Vassilli, the woodcutter," answered the rabbi, "I'm selling firewood."

"Please go away," called the woman. "I have no money for firewood."

"Oh, that doesn't matter," said the rabbi cheerfully. "I'll lend you the money."

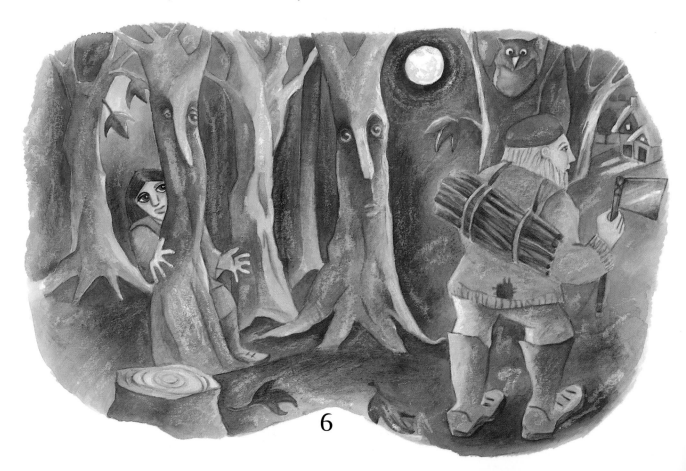

The woman coughed. She was obviously very sick. "I may not be able to pay you back for a long time."

"I can wait," said the rabbi. He opened the door and carried the wood inside the house.

"But who's going to light the fire?" asked the woman.

"I will," said the rabbi.

The boy, watching from the window, saw him place the wood in the stove. As he worked, he recited the first part of the special Yom Kippur prayer. Then, as he lit the fire, he said the second part. When the fire was roaring away, he recited the third and last part.

"Thank you, Vassilli," said the woman gratefully.

 7

The rabbi shut the stove and, bidding the sick lady a good year, he ran back home to change. The boy hurried on to the synagogue before him.

"And where on Earth is the rabbi?" complained one of the faithful. "He hasn't shown his face all night. It's nearly dawn."

"He's not anywhere on Earth, dear," said her friend. "He's in heaven, talking to God."

The boy, who'd overheard every word, shook his head. "He's not in heaven either. He's somewhere much higher than that."

8

Sephardic Nut Cookies

Sephardic Jews are of Spanish and Portuguese descent.
Many of them live in the Middle East. Here is a Sephardic recipe
for nut cookies. They are eaten on the evening of Yom Kippur
(after the fast is over) or for Sabbath breakfasts.

Makes 10–12 cookies

1 cup plain flour
1 tsp baking powder
pinch of salt
2 eggs

3 tbsp sugar
3 tbsp vegetable oil
few drops vanilla extract
handful chopped almonds

1 Sift the flour and the baking powder. Mix together in a bowl with the pinch of salt.
2 Beat one of the eggs with the sugar, oil, and vanilla.
3 Add the flour and mix to make a dough.
4 Roll the dough into strands, about 0.5 in. (1.25 cm) thick and 6 in. (15 cm) long. Make these strands into rings and prick with a fork.
5 Beat the second egg. Dip one side of the rings into it and then sprinkle with the chopped nuts.
6 Place well apart on a greased baking tray. Preheat the oven to 375 °F and bake the cookies for 20 minutes or until golden brown.

WARNING: Do not bake the cookies without an adult's help. The oven will get very hot and you could get burned.

I Have a Little Dreidel

Hanukkah is the festival of light. It reminds us of the time when the Jewish people reclaimed the temple of Jerusalem from the enemy. Today people celebrate Hanukkah by lighting candles in a holder called a Menorah. They also play games with a spinning top called a dreidel. Here's a famous dreidel song.

I have a lit - tle drei - del,   I made it out of clay;   And

when it's dry and ready   Then drei - del   I shall play.   O

drei - del drei - del drei - del,   I made it out of clay;   O

drei - del drei - del drei - del,   Now drei - del   I shall play.

1 I have a little dreidel
  I made it out of clay
  And when it's dry and ready
  Then dreidel I shall play!

    Chorus
    Oh dreidel, dreidel, dreidel
    I made it out of clay
    And when it's dry and ready
    Then dreidel I shall play!

2 It has a lovely body
  With legs so short and thin
  And when my dreidel's tired
  It drops and then I win!

    Chorus
    Oh dreidel, dreidel, dreidel, etc

3 My dreidel's always playful
  It loves to dance and spin
  A happy game of dreidel
  Come play now, let's begin.

    Chorus
    Oh dreidel, dreidel, dreidel, etc

The Best Purim Ever

Purim celebrates the day when Queen Esther saved the Jewish people from Haman, a wicked courtier who wanted to destroy all the Jews in Persia.

Jacob and his friends were very excited. It was Purim and they had all made special rattles called graggers to use in the temple.

"Now don't forget," said Rachel, Jacob's best friend. "We mustn't talk while the rabbi is reading us the story of how Esther saved the Jews, but we're allowed to rattle our graggers every time he mentions the evil courtier Haman."

"Like this," said Jacob, and he spun his gragger.

His friends put their hands over their ears. "That must be the loudest gragger in the world," gasped Rachel.

Jacob's papa came into the room.

"I need to speak to all of you," he said.

The children put down their graggers.

"The prince may die," said Papa.

The children gasped. Earlier in the week the czar's son had become lost in the forest while hunting. Some woodcutters had led him to the safety of Vardik, the little Russian town where they lived. The people of Vardik had given the prince the best room at the inn. The innkeeper had cooked him a splendid meal. But, at night, the prince had fallen ill. His attendants had brought the czar and his doctors. The doctors insisted that the Jewish people of Vardik had given the prince bad food. Everyone in Vardik knew that wasn't true, of course. The innkeeper had given the czar's son good food.

"Now the czar has said that if the prince dies, we shall all be punished," said Jacob's Papa. "Meanwhile, the doctors say that no one is to make any noise at all. The prince is unconscious and might never wake up again."

"Can't we even take our graggers to the temple tonight?" asked Jacob.

"You must leave your graggers at home," said Papa. "The temple is right next to the inn." The children obeyed; all except Jacob, who smuggled his gragger into the temple hidden under his coat.

The rabbi started reading the story of Esther. He spoke in a whisper, so that only people in the temple could hear him. "Everyone liked Queen Esther," he said, "everyone except the evil Haman."

As soon as the rabbi mentioned Haman, Jacob whipped out his gragger and twirled it around. The noise was deafening, and everyone in the temple gasped. The rabbi looked horrified, but went on reading. But soon he mentioned Haman again, and again Jacob spun his champion gragger. Now everyone looked frightened, because the doctors were glaring at the congregation from the prince's window next door. Papa hissed at Jacob to stop, but the naughty boy didn't put the gragger away. Instead he spun it around again.

 15

In the prince's room, the czar came to the window. "Who is making that awful noise?" he asked.

"It's a boy in the temple," said a doctor.

"Tell him to be quiet," ordered the king, "or I'll have him put in prison."

Just then there was a rustling of sheets behind him. "Papa?" asked a weak voice, "what is that noise?"

The czar stiffened: the prince had woken up.

"I heard a funny noise," said the prince. "It sounded like the rattle you gave me for my birthday once." He turned to a doctor. "Bring me some water. I am thirsty."

One of the servants ran out on to the street. "The prince has woken up," she cried. "The prince is getting better. We are safe!"

Everyone in the temple sighed with relief. Then they started to beam at Jacob. His gragger had woken the prince.

"Well done, boy," said the rabbi. "You have saved our lives. Now we can have the best Purim ever."

Jacob smiled proudly. And then he raised his gragger in the air and twirled it around once more.

Had Gadya

During Pesach (Passover), Jewish people celebrate the time when their ancestors escaped from slavery in Egypt to look for the promised land. They have a special feast called a Seder meal, at the end of which they sing songs like this.

One kid, just one kid.
My father bought for two zuzim, one kid,
just one kid.

Then came a cat and ate the kid
that my father bought for two zuzim,
Had gadya, had gadya.

Then came a dog and bit the cat
   that ate the kid
that my father bought for two zuzim,
Had gadya, had gadya.

18

Then came a stick and beat the dog
    that bit the cat that ate the kid
that my father bought for two zuzim,
Had gadya, had gadya.

Then came a fire and burned the stick
    That beat the dog that bit the cat that ate the kid
that my father bought for two zuzim,
Had gadya, had gadya.

Then came water and quenched the fire
    that burned the stick that beat the dog
    that bit the cat that ate the kid
that my father bought for two zuzim,
Had gadya, had gadya.

Then came an ox and drank the water
    that quenched the fire that burned the stick
    that beat the dog that bit the cat that ate the kid
that my father bought for two zuzim,
Had gadya, had gadya.

Then came a shohet and slaughtered the ox
    that drank the water that quenched the fire
    that burned the stick that beat the dog
    that bit the cat that ate the kid
that my father bought for two zuzim,
Had gadya, had gadya.

Then came the angel of death who killed the shohet
    who slaughtered the ox that drank the water
    that quenched the fire that burned the stick
    that beat the dog that bit the cat that ate the kid
that my father bought for two zuzim,
Had gadya, had gadya.

Then came the Holy One and killed the angel of death
    who killed the shohet
    who slaughtered the ox
    that drank the water
    that quenched the fire
    that burned the stick
    that beat the dog
    that bit the cat
    that ate the kid
that my father bought for two zuzim,
Had gadya, had gadya.

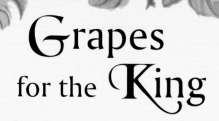

Grapes
for the King

Shavuot is two celebrations in one. It is a harvest festival as well as a commemoration of the time when God gave the Jewish people the ten commandments. In ancient times, it was called Yom Habbikkurim or "the day of the first fruits" because that was the day when the farmers took the first fruits of the harvest for a blessing ritual in the temple of Jerusalem.

Cast of Characters

Simon, a boy

Anna, his sister

Elizabeth, his mother

Rebecca, his best friend

Ruth, Elizabeth's best friend

A king

Attendants

Farmers

Flute players

Dancers

Scene 1: A farm just outside Jerusalem.

We can see fig trees and grapevines with lots of ribbons tied to the branches. To the right side is a wooden hen coop. It is sunrise. Anna comes in with a basket. She looks at a grapevine, sees some fruit, and ties a ribbon around it. Then she goes into the coop and starts feeding the hens.

Anna: Here you are chickens, chick, chick, chick.

Enter Simon, with firewood under his right arm.
He sees the ripening grapes, drops the wood, and is about
to pick some, when Anna rushes out of the coop.

Anna: Ma, Simon is going to pick the first grapes!
Simon: I was only having a look.

Elizabeth comes rushing onstage.

Elizabeth: What's going on?
Anna: Simon was going to pick the first grapes.
Elizabeth: Now, Simon, you know we have to leave those for the festival. All the first fruits on the farm have to be blessed at the temple.

Simon: I was only going to have a look at them.
Anna: You weren't. You were going to pick them.
Elizabeth: Anna, don't shout. [*She takes a ribbon from her pocket and ties it around a bunch of figs.*] There, now we can be sure to leave the first figs alone, too.

23

Simon: It's very silly, if you ask me. Tying ribbons around fruit. Why can't we just eat them?

Elizabeth: Because, Simon, God sent us that fruit and all the other crops on the farm. And we must thank Him by taking the first fruit of each kind to the temple in Jerusalem. Don't you want to come to Jerusalem, Simon?

Simon: Of course I do. Not to offer the first fruit, though. I want to meet the king.

Anna: Meet the king? As if the king would want to meet you.

Simon: He might, when I tell him I want to join the army.

Anna: [*laughing*]: You, join the army?

Elizabeth: Now, Anna, don't laugh at your brother. Bring in those eggs and you, Simon, pick up that firewood. Your papa might be home from the pastures today.

Exit Elizabeth and Anna. Simon starts picking up the firewood.

Simon: I wish I was the king, then I wouldn't have to carry anything at all.

Enter his friend Rebecca.

Rebecca: Hello, Simon, are you going to the festival tomorrow?

Simon: I don't think I have a choice.

Rebecca: Come on, it'll be fun.

Simon: If you call lugging baskets of fruit around fun.

Rebecca: I'm going. I'll walk with you, if you like.

Simon: That would be great, as long as you don't make me dance.

Rebecca: I promise I won't. [*Laughs, but kindly.*] A mule can dance better than you, Simon.

Simon: I'm hoping to meet the king.

Rebecca: How will you recognize him?

Simon: By his clothes, of course. He must be covered in jewels. And he'll have a golden crown on his head. And a sword. He'll definitely have a sword.

Elizabeth [*calling offstage*]: Simon, bring in that wood.

Simon: I must go. Mother's calling me.

Rebecca: See you tomorrow, then.

Simon: See you.

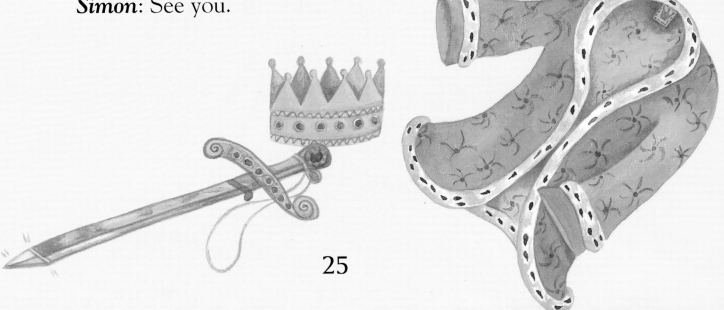

25

They both exit. Change of light. Music. Enter the crowd. Everyone carries baskets of fruit and vegetables. All the produce is decorated with ribbons. Some carry wine and olive jars. There is a festive spirit in the air. Simon, Anna, Rebecca, and Elizabeth join the crowd.

Rebecca [*to Simon*]: This is fun, isn't it?

Anna: Have you seen the king yet?

Simon: Not yet, but I'm sure I will.

Elizabeth: Simon, carry that basket properly. Put it on your head.

Simon: Can't Anna carry it for me?

Elizabeth: Anna already has her own basket to carry.

Rebecca [*teasing Simon*]: I bet the king doesn't have to carry a basket.

Elizabeth: The king will meet us at the temple steps. He will carry a basket of fruit from there into the temple himself.

Simon: But he doesn't have to carry it all the way along the road in the hot sun.

Ruth, a friend of Elizabeth, spots them.

Ruth: Elizabeth, I haven't seen you for a long time!

Elizabeth: Ruth!

They embrace.

26

Someone jostles Simon, and the fruit falls out of his basket and scatters all over the floor. Simon starts to pick up the fruit while the crowd moves offstage.

Elizabeth: Simon, you must take better care of the harvest. Pick up all that fruit and catch up with us. Come on. Anna, Rebecca, we mustn't dawdle. Ruth, tell me about your children. Are they helping out on the farm yet?

Simon is left alone onstage. Enter the king, who is dressed like a farmer.

King: Can I help you?
Simon: Thank you.

The king picks up some fruit and puts it in Simon's basket.

King: You grow some nice fruit.
Simon: My mother's very proud of her grapes. Have you no fruit?
King: I'm afraid not.
Simon: You're lucky. You don't have to walk around with a basket on your head.
King: Perhaps I am lucky.
Simon: I wish I was the king, then I wouldn't have to carry anything.

King: I think even the king has to carry something, sometimes.

Simon: I bet his servants do all the carrying for him.

King: I'll carry the basket for you, if you want.

Simon: Thanks.

They start walking, the king with the basket on his head. Crowds come in again.

A man: We've reached the walls of Jerusalem.

A woman: Our journey is over.

The king's servants rush in. One of them carries a golden basket decorated with jewels and ribbons. It is filled with a lot of fruit, but no grapes.

Servant: Your Majesty, we have been looking everywhere for you. The priests are waiting.

King: I wanted to walk with the farmers, just for a short while, to show God that I too am thankful for His harvest, even if I do not have time to grow my own crops.

Servant: We've brought you a basket of fruit, Your Majesty.

The king gives Simon's basket back to him. The servant hands the king the grand basket.

28

King: Thank you for letting me share your harvest, friend. I was lucky to meet you.

Simon: [*lost for words*]: You, you're …

King: May I take some of your grapes? I'll offer them to God as if they were mine.

The king exits with his servants. Elizabeth, Ruth, Rebecca, and Anna enter.

Elizabeth: Simon, where have you been? We were worried you might have run off back home.

Simon: Don't be silly, Mother. I am proud to carry my basket.

Anna: You, proud to carry a basket? I thought you wanted to be the king.

Simon: Even the king has to carry something, sometimes, you know. Come on, let's hurry up. I want to thank God for giving us such beautiful grapes. They're fit for a king.

Music. They all exit.

Festival Information

The Jewish calendar has 12 months. Each month has 29 or 30 days. During Jewish leap years there is a 13th month. (A leap year occurs at irregular intervals, seven times in a 19-year cycle.) The Jewish New Year starts on the seventh month, called Tishri. But, according to an old custom, the year is counted from Nisan, the first month.

ROSH HASHANAH is considered by many to be the beginning of the Jewish New Year. It is also the start of the ten High Holy Days that end with Yom Kippur, the day of atonement. Unlike other Jewish holidays, these two are purely religious and do not commemorate a historical event.

During Rosh Hashanah, families gather together to eat special foods. Some of these are sweet, to make sure that the coming year will be a sweet one. Many start the first night's meal by eating apple slices or *challah* bread dipped in honey.

Rosh Hashanah is also a time for prayer, when people look at the past year and ask God to forgive them their shortcomings. In the temple, a respected member of the community blows a ram's horn called a *shofar*. The sound reminds people that they should strive to lead better lives. It is customary to give money to charity during Rosh Hoshahna.

YOM KIPPUR is the last day of the ten High Holy Days. It is the holiest day in the Jewish calendar and many people call it the "Sabbath of Sabbaths."

The night before Yom Kippur, people eat a hearty meal because the next day they have to fast. They gather in the temple to recite a special prayer called the *Kol Nidrei*. It is repeated three times, each time in a louder voice. Men wear special prayer shawls. During the service, people say they are sorry for their sins and assure God that they will not break their promises to him again.

Eating, drinking, washing, and wearing leather shoes are all prohibited on Yom Kippur. At the end of the day, the *shofar* is blown and everyone in the temple shouts "Next year in Jerusalem!" Then everyone heads home for a special feast.

HANUKKAH is the "festival of lights." It commemorates the time when the Jews won the Jerusalem temple back from the Greeks and re-dedicated it.

The Greeks had conquered the Jews and were forcing many of them to give up their religion and worship Greek gods. They filled the temple in Jerusalem with statues of Greek gods. Judah the Macabee and his brothers led a revolt against the Greeks. After three years of fighting, the Jews won. After they had cleaned the temple, the Macabees wanted to rekindle the "eternal light." But there was only enough oil in the lamp for one day. Someone was sent to get more oil, but it took them eight days to come back. Miracuously, the lamp in the temple continued to burn for all that time. To remind people of that, the Hanukkah festival lasts eight days.

Most Jewish people celebrate Hanukkah at home. They have special food, sing songs, and light a nine-branched candlestick called a menorah.

During Hanukkah, children play with a small spinning top called a dreidel. It has a Hebrew letter written on each of the four sides. At the time of the Macabees, Jewish people were not allowed to study their religion, and it is said that the dreidel game was invented to hide such study. The Hebrew letters spell out the initials of the phrase "a great miracle happened there." To play the game, a player spins the dreidel and, depending on which letter the dreidel lands on, wins or loses a token.

PURIM During this festival people celebrate the day when Queen Esther and her brave uncle Mordecai saved the Jewish people from slaughter at the hands of the king of Persia. The story is told in the "Book Of Esther," known as the *Megillah*. In the story, Haman hated the Jews and convinced the king to kill them all. He drew lots, or purim, to decide which day the slaughter was to take place. This gave the festival its name. Jewish people listen to the story in the temple during Purim. Every time the name of Haman is mentioned, they boo and twirl special rattles called graggers.

During Purim, children put on masks and dress up as characters from the Esther story. Jewish people give gifts or money to at least two poor people. They also present friends and family with a basket of fruit. One of the sweets eaten during Purim is a three-cornered pastry modeled on Haman's hat.

6th day—Shavuot

PESACH (also known as Passover) celebrates the day when the Jews escaped slavery in Egypt to find "the promised land." The celebrations last eight days, during which time families gather for celebratory meals and the reading of the *Haggadah*, which tells the story of the escape of the Jewish people from Egypt.

The main celebration meal of the Passover is called the Seder and takes place on the first two nights of the festival. It is an eleborate ritual with special foods and activities. Before Passover, Jewish people clean their houses and get rid of all foods with yeast in them. Special pans, dishes, and utensils are taken out of storage and used to cook the Seder meal.

Only foods without any yeast are allowed for the Passover celebration. This reminds people that the Jewish slaves did not have time to let their dough rise before baking bread for the journey to the promised land.

During the meal, the door to the house is left open to welcome in the prophet Elijah. Songs are sung.

Afterward children join in a hunt around the house for a special type of unleavened bread, or matzah, which is called the *Afikomen*. When it is found, it is shared by everyone.

SHAVUOT commemorates the giving of the ten commandments to Moses. It is also a Spring festival. There are many traditions surrounding the holiday.

Legend has it that the Jewish people in the desert fell asleep while waiting for the ten commandments. So now they stay up all night before Shavuot studying the Torah. The custom is called *Tikun Lail Shavuot*.

Particular dairy products, such as cheesecake, are eaten for Shavuot. Homes and temples are decorated with flowers and greenery. This is partly to celebrate the Spring aspect of the festival but also to remind people of an old legend. It is said that when Moses received the ten commandments, the desert burst into bloom to help the people rejoice.

Glossary

Ax A very sharp tool for cutting wood.

Congregation A group of people who have come together in a synagogue or temple.

Coop A cage for chickens.

Courtier Someone who waits on or works for a king.

Czar The ruler of Russia.

Dawn The first light of the day, when the sun comes up.

Dreidel A small spinning top.

Gragger A very noisy rattle.

Inn A place where people could stay when they were away from home.

Heaven The place where God and angels are believed to be, usually thought of as beyond the sky.

Kid A baby goat.

Ox A general name for animals such as cows or buffalo.

Prayers Talking to God, by asking things, or saying thank you. Sometimes people pray silently.

Rabbi A Jewish leader and teacher.

Synagogue Building where Jewish people people meet and pray.

Temple Place where people meet to worship a god or gods.

Unconscious Not aware of surroundings or people nearby. Usually happens when someone is very sick.

Index

Resources

Books

Bracken, Thomas. *Good Luck Symbols and Talismans*. New York: Chelsea House, 1997.

Clark, Anne, et al. *Hanukkah* (World of Holidays). Austin, TX: Raintree Steck-Vaughn, 1998.

Fine, Doreen. *What Do We Know About Judaism*. Peter Bedrick, 1996.

Haskins, James. *Count Your Way Through Israel*. New York: First Avenue Editions, 1992.

Slim, Hugo. *A Feast of Festivals*. New York: HarperCollins, 1996.

Waldman, Neil. *The Golden City: Jerusalem's 3,000 Years*. New York: Atheneum, 1995.

——. *Masada*. New York: Morrow Junior Books, 1998.

Videos

The Prince of Egypt (Dreamworks, 1999) is an animated film that tells the story of Moses and the Passover.

Web sites

www.anjy.org
  Jewish youth web site with a variety of activities, including finding penfriends, Jewish resources and games.
www.jewishmuseum.org
  The web site of New York's Jewish Museum: opens a window on to the history and religious life of the Jewish community in America and beyond.
www.jewish.com/
  Information, news, shopping, music, etc.